Being American after the Destruction of Gaza

A Letter to Pope Leo XIV

Donald G. Boland

En Route Books and Media, LLC
Saint Louis, MO

⊕*ENROUTE*
Make the time

En Route Books and Media, LLC

5705 Rhodes Avenue

St. Louis, MO 63109

Cover credit: Jesus weeping over Jerusalem,
generated by DALL-E

ISBN-13: 979-8-88870-396-0

Library of Congress Control Number: 2025942574

Dedicated

to

Blessed Clemens August Cardinal von Galen
"The Lion of Munster"

There is a readily available book entitled "The Lion of Munster" in which can be found a full account of the life and work of the remarkable Clemens August von Galen. So there is no need to set out any details of the heroic German bishop here.

Quotations

"Thou shalt not kill." (5th Commandment)

"by their fruits you shall know them" (Matt. 7:16)

"And when he drew near, seeing the city, he wept over it, saying: If thou also hadst known, and that in this thy day, the things that are to thy peace; but now they are hidden from thy eyes." (Luke 19; 41,42).

"The problem with our communal story is not that it acknowledges the crimes we have suffered. The problem is that it ignores the crimes we commit." (Peter Beinart: *Being Jewish After the Destruction of Gaza: A Reckoning.*)

Table of Contents

Being American after the Destruction of Gaza

A Letter to Pope Leo XIV

To be fair, it is rather premature to be writing to the new pope when it is hardly more than a few weeks since he was elected. The title of this essay may then be taken as a catchy way of drawing attention to what is said in it, which relates to the position of the papacy as it appears to stand at the present time. We will need to see whether the present pope continues in the same vein or makes what some may see as a necessary correction. Many positions concerned are not clear and it may be a matter of clarification than correction.

I mean here to focus on only one matter of concern, which I see is probably the most urgent and important for clarity at least to be had, that is to say, as to how oneself not just as Catholic but also human, should judge the matter in question and act in good conscience.

In fact, this letter has been prompted by a piece published in *La Civilta Cattolica* in the last few days. That (Jesuit) publication claims to represent the mind of the Vatican (dating back to 1850). Whether or not that is so, what we are concerned to know is the position of the papacy. The piece mentioned is on a recent book: *Being Jewish after the Destruction of Gaza: A Reckoning* by Peter Beinart.

The comment on the book is: Beinart's fourth book, *Being Jewish After the Destruction of Gaza: A Reckoning*, was released in January 2025. In it, he argues that "Jewish texts, history, and language have been deployed to justify mass slaughter and starvation [of the population of Gaza]".

The book commented upon is a powerful one. The accusation made in the quote from it could not be more damning of the actions of the Israeli State in Gaza and the attempts by members of the Jewish community to defend such actions. What is to be noted however, and it is the basic point of my letter, is that the same accusation must be levelled also at the USA (and by extension at the West generally); not just in the actions of its leadership, but in the behaviour of those citizens who not only fail to condemn but also actively defend the Israeli State's mass slaughter and starvation of the population of Gaza - which is so public that only the blind (who will not to see) would deny it.

The State of Israel does not deny its actions nor hide its intent. Beinart writes to persuade his own Jewish community, wherever they may live, if mainly in the USA. He does not go into the complicity of his own country (USA) in the carrying out of such mass slaughter and starvation policy. That is what I wish to bring out in my letter to Pope Leo XIV, who incidentally is a citizen of the USA.

One cannot trust the media of course as it is a vehicle of propaganda by all countries, especially their governments. But under the previous Pope Francis I did not notice any outright condemnation coming from the Vatican of either the State of Israel or "America". Indeed, in my view the US is more culpable inasmuch as the scale of the slaughter (including many helpless Palestinian mothers and their children) is only possible with the use of monstrous munitions supplied from "America". The US has the additional shameful culpability of staying out of direct involvement like a coward urging others to do what it would not want to be seen doing itself. However these are points I wish to develop later in my "letter".

The book's author is evidently a person of strong character and in the points he argues one of unusual courage. The general position he takes is in direct opposition to that which he had previously taken strongly, but now involves vehement opposition from his friends and even relatives belonging to the same Jewish religion to which he still adheres. It is clearly a matter of conscience, in fact a prise de conscience that has wrenched his soul after much struggle.

The issue however is quite clear cut; only made not so by deep seated emotional factors - loyalty to religion, family, country. The clarity exists at the level of a common human nature. Are Palestinians, in Gaza, of equal human dignity as Jews or anyone else are, especially when each is competing for the same homeland?

We do not wish to go into the event (on 7th October) leading up to the actions of the Israeli State and armed forces. Regardless of the crimes committed on that day we are concerned with the events that followed on the part of the State of Israel. One who commits crimes will be tempted to justify them by pointing to the offenses committed against him. This is quite irrelevant to the assessment of one's guilt for action taken on one's own behalf. It is quite evident that this deceitful ploy has been made great use of in this case, seemingly to great effect.

I will put the matter in terms that have been used by those who we may regard as independent investigators, such as Professor John Mearsheimer and Professor Jeffrey Sachs.

A "breakout" of what the Palestinians and others regarded as a concentration camp (an eerie analogy) occurred. This was taken by the Israeli government (State) as a reason or opportunity to justify the full capture of the coastal strip of territory called Gaza. This has now become plain if it was represented originally as the extermination of the group Hamas. The project is tied to the notion of "Greater Israel"? Emotion takes over, and "war" is declared to be against Hamas, the group that in fact rules the territory so far as Palestinians are concerned. But it is obviously more than that.

The Palestinians involved in the day of "breakout" were described by a senior member of the Israeli government as being "human animals" (eerily reminiscent of the mass murder of the Jewish race being justified by a Nazi official as the elimination of a sub-human pestilence).

Whatever be the causes, it has become clear to many, including those in the USA of the highest international reputation, expertise and integrity, such as professors John Mearsheimer and Jeffrey Sachs (the latter a Jew himself, as well as a member of the Pontifical Academy of Social Sciences), that the Israeli State and its "Defence Force" (IDF) have gone well beyond the bounds of the laws of international conflict and indeed have been guilty, and continue to be guilty, of the most criminal activity (mass destruction of innocent human life, a good proportion being women and their children of tender age) carried out in great part with bombs from planes liberally provided by the USA - which brings in the question of complicity in crimes against humanity.

The professors mentioned are prepared to put these crimes as heinous acts of "ethnic cleansing" and genocide. There seems little doubt that these actions are planned.

However, leaving these assessments of the situation aside it is evident that Peter Beinart is not alone among Jews in the USA coming to realise that what they can see being perpetrated in Gaza as it were in their name cannot be justified. Indeed, the action of the Israeli State is an affront to their consciences. Some whose relatives suffered in the Holocaust have come out in protest. Beinart is but one whose public image has a prominence that cannot be ignored or swept aside by propaganda of powerful supporters of Israel.

If his condemnation is just, and one who observes what has been presented to the eyes of everyone day by day must agree it is, then it is hard to understand how people can view the situation and not be horrified by the mass slaughter of innocent civilians and destruction of non military buildings of a whole population by the dropping of bombs on such a massive scale.

As stated, the above is a preliminary expression of the contents of the article/letter I propose to write.

Peter Beinart puts at the end of the title of his book the word "A Reckoning". This is obviously put in the moral sense that the word has of rendering an account of one's behaviour, actions and omissions, which reckoning may take place in this world (as at Nuremberg) but in any case the account must be rendered to God at death and the last judgment.

The word "reckon" originally had the meaning the same as think or judge, but then taken in the mathematical sense of rendering an account in monetary terms. But it acquired a broader and even moral sense as noted above. This is obviously the meaning in which Beinart uses it. And since he is a fervently religious Jew, it even takes on the seriousness of a judgment on the state of one's soul, and, if guilty of serious sin, refers to behaviour that needs either to be repented of, to obtain divine mercy, or to suffer damnation and just punishment. The Christian is in the same state of mind, which is relevant to any complicity of Catholics in the US (or by extension in those who side with the US in the matter). However, since the crimes (mostly of murder) are evidently against the Natural Moral Law, no one as a human being can escape blame and punishment for their complicity in any crime against humanity.

Thus it is that everyone in the West who, aware of the criminal behaviour of the US, does not condemn but supports it (such as Australians), is in the same morally perilous position. They all face a similar reckoning that Beinart refers to for his own Jewish community with regard to the State of Israel.

That makes the point of our letter from a personal point of view. What we wish to go into however is how the situation may be affected with regard to one in the position of religious authority, and in particular a pope. This is why these thoughts of mine have taken the form of a letter to the present pope. For, on first impression, as noted, I have not seen any outright condemnation of the actions of the State of Israel or of the USA, coming from the papacy or the Vatican. There is much expression of compassion for the people of Gaza and for the need for peace or ceasefire in the "war" where innocent Palestinians are being slaughtered and starved as one speaks. But so far as I am aware there have been no expressions of righteous anger and of the courage of public condemnation at the murderous assaults made on non-combatants and the wholesale destruction of homes and ordinary buildings. It is to be remembered that the US has supplied and is continually supplying the means of mass destruction. One deceitful tactic used, as we have noted above, is to attempt to excuse one's course of criminal action by pointing to a criminal action against oneself in the past. Another is to point to hateful comments made, as if they were against Jews generally when they are prompted in many cases by the offenses of some. Beinart has a chapter on affected charges of antisemitism in his book.

So far as the papacy is concerned there are of course considerations that affect what it does or declines to do. Pope Pius XII is criticised for not condemning Hitler or the Nazi government. Circumstances may counsel silence as they did in his case. Then there is the fact that as Christ himself said, his Kingdom and hence the Church is not of this world. Pope Benedict XVI pointed out that justice is a matter for human political governments and the Church will not take over what States should do. The assessment of papal intervention has some special complications.

However, most of these considerations of course do not come into play where nations and their political leaders and populace are concerned. At the level of human affairs it is not enough for one to say "we are only concerned with our national interest". One has a duty to go to the aid of a stranger, and another civil community, in peril if one can. Failure to do so will be taken into account on the day of reckoning, which runs immediately upon the failure.

One needs to listen then to Peter Beinart and to other Jews, like Jeffrey Sachs and Norman Finkelstein. At the human level of natural moral law and obligation, it is the ones who rightly condemn and protest at the criminal behaviour of the State of Israel and the complicity of the USA who need not fear the day of reckoning.

But I wish to look a little more closely at what Catholic clerics, from priest to bishop to pope, should be doing. What I propose to do is take a look at what was done by a German Catholic bishop, Clemens von Galen, during the Nazi era of the last century and see what instruction we can take from how he addressed the same sort of horrific situation. There are of course important differences between that time and ours but the issues are at root strangely the same despite the incredible reversal of roles.

In order to have but the slightest insight into the situation of Bishop von Galen during the Nazi regime in Germany one needs to appreciate that anyone living at any time would have a history that goes back to Adam and Eve, through a multitude of ancestors from a particular religious and ethnic origin, developing to various kinds of civil or political communities through eventually to a primitive society, or civilized nation or state of the modern era. Man is not only a political animal, as Aristotle noted, but also a religious, and properly domestic animal. It is a peculiar feature of late modern times that the political aspect of human nature has come to so dominate individuals' lives and affairs that these three distinct orders and communities to which individual persons belong naturally have become, as it were, homogenized into one. That is the political, and that in a most unnatural and even monstrous form. It has grown to enormous proportions within which are gross party and ideological divisions on a global scale.

The supernatural community which is the Church founded by Christ would seem to have sparked in the human mind the idea of a world political community (like to Christendom). But this was sought to be realised as a secular idea only after the Church's divine authority was rejected in a series of revolutions centred in the religious one called the Protestant Reformation.

There has always been a radical state of war between human individuals and groups, and even within the individual human heart, which the Christian will trace back to original sin. Even after the coming of Christ whereby this sinful condition has been cured by grace, there remain effects of original sin on human nature so that apart from Christ and his mother no one can say he is without sin in this life. This sinful condition even with the continuing presence of the Holy Church and her community of saints has grown in force so much that the modern era has descended to a state of decline of Faith and corruption of morals that is worse than ever. There is of course an explanation for this in divine providence. But many have a sense of impending doom.

From a natural point of view there is plenty of "reason" for such despair. The all but victory of the forces of evil in political and military terms, driven by ideologies such as Nazism, Fascism and Communism in the last century, have changed the previous optimistic mood (fuelled by power over nature by modern science and technology). It has dissipated, if the defeat of those forces of evil brought a revival of confidence and hope for the future of mankind. But such was short-lived. Men and women of wisdom have come to realise that the evil ideologies are deep seated in modern thought and political practice and have returned with greater force in ways quite unexpected and alarming.

We focus here only on the ideology of Nazism. We mean to consider the resistance to it by Bishop von Galen. However, as he did, we abstract as best we can from its peculiar Germanic form, and the bizarre theories connected with it such as Hitler's notion of the purity and superiority of the Aryan race. As we shall see, even the selection of the Jewish ethnic character is a feature, that comes from a flawed reading of human history, that is not essential to the irrationality of the political ideology.

This has an important bearing on our assessment of the current situation involving the actions of the State of Israel and its treatment of the population of Gaza, as well as involving the support given by the USA.

As Bishop von Galen saw, the deep fault in the ideology is its assumption of absolute power by the State, adopted by any particular political institution, and its consequent belief it has the right to treat another people who oppose it as somehow subhuman and worthy of extermination if necessary. When it was put to a German State Official that all men are of equal dignity he said No: In the case of the Jews it was a matter of elimination of a "pestilence" that it was necessary to destroy for the security of the German nation, and by extension of the human race as a whole. Hitler could draw on the history of Europe and the troubled relationship between the Church and the Jews to justify discrimination against them as a race. This was a theological complicating factor that allowed the Nazis to gain ground in Germany.

We might insert here a comment on the philosophical error that underlies this political ideology.

It comes from the denial of the superiority of the natural moral law over positive law, or to put it in another way, the denial of the principles of personal ethics (and conscience) being more fundamental than political or civic ethics, and domestic ethics.

We refer the readers to our books on Ethics where it is shown that there are three orders and three common goods. The political common good is not the highest. St. Thomas points out that man is not subject to the common good of the civil community in all that he is. Aristotle points out to think so would be to make man the most supreme being instead of God. So it is that in the modern era with the rejection first of the Church of Christ and ultimately of religion itself, it is quasi natural for men to make themselves, whether individually or collectively, the highest form of reality (identified with human freedom taken as absolute). That is the basis of the two dominant ideologies of Individualistic/capitalism and collectivistic socialism, each appropriating to itself the championing of absolutist freedom, for which Liberalism is but another name. Hence the confusing use of liberalism by both ideologies.

Von Galen eventually saw Nazism as a disguised form of State Absolutism. Italian Fascism is but another form of State Absolutism. Von Galen already saw Soviet Communism as a form of State absolutism of a most violent and murderous kind where the individual person counts as dispensable to the perceived interests of the State.

There are various peculiar historical features that attach to both kinds of ideologies. In modern times it is the division between the few rich and the many poor, taking the form of those who have commandeered (by robbery and deceit) virtually all right to property (backed by legal positivism), and come to be called Capitalism, as against the majority thereby being made politically impotent by being reduced to a state of propertyless proletarianism (the word comes from proles meaning orphaned).

The majority is then made to become the workers paid a wage in money, "backed" by property in wealth that includes the capital (technical instruments) necessary to produce by Labour. However, we cannot go into such details here. They are dealt with in my previous books.

In the beginning it was only after the basic ideology of Nazism became clear that the Church and the papacy, and even von Galen, moved strongly to condemn the new German Reich (political government). To the German people the situation of extermination of Jews en masse was somewhat hidden early because it began first in Poland. The most evident early feature of the regime in Germany was its attack on the Catholic Church and its Institutions, such as education.

It is to be remembered also that Hitler came to power fully in 1933, and the Second World War began in 1939. Von Galen was ordained bishop of Munster in October 1933. The situation developed - for the worse - rapidly and Pope Pius XI's famous encyclical condemning Nazism was published in 1937. Von Galen is reported to have had a part in its composition.

We need to keep in mind that the period of the modern world in Europe after the Protestant Reformation and the other revolutions that accompanied it was of the utmost turbulence. The new nations began with wars, and like England under Henry VIII, with wholesale murder and plunder, setting up new nation states ruled by what St. Augustine would describe as bands of robbers, who over time gained the respectability of established rulers.

The philosophy of law of all new nation states was firmly based in positivist legal philosophy making the regime, if operating under the form of a Parliament, but a disguised form of absolute rule.

This remains the basis of all modern states today (including USA, UK and Israel - if the last confirms its positivist character by claiming it as divinely based). The language of being under God is used but in the USA for instance they are the words of a humanly formed Constitution that was and is taken as more fundamental than the Natural Moral Law or even the Ten Commandments. But we must stay with the situation in Europe and Germany.

Bishop von Galen was not initially opposed to the new Government under Hitler. In June 1933 he called for a just and objective evaluation of Hitler's new political movement. Nor was he particularly sympathetic to the situation of the Jews in Germany. They were not all poor working class. Coming to know of Hitler's mass slaughter of them changed all antipathy against them. The use that the present State of Israel has made of this is something that Peter Beinart discusses in his chapter on Antisemitism.

However we need to look more closely at how the Bishop of Munster resisted, to the point of public condemnation, the politics of Hitler and the Nazi government of Germany.

For the purposes of this letter/article I do not intend to go into the record of the bishop's criticism of the Nazi regime in all its aspects. Nor would I attempt to discuss the papal interventions, or lack of same, during the period of Nazi rule in Germany. It is rather idle to do so since the actual contingencies of the times are too much for someone not living through them to make any fair judgment on actions or omissions by the parties in the thick of things.

One is better served by considering the character of the persons involved and, if viewed as of fundamental goodness, being ready to believe that they judged things according to virtues such as prudence, rather than vices such as cowardice.

I am here more concerned to assess a current situation in which we are all involved and which requires us to make similarly difficult decisions and evaluate as best we can the decisions to be made by others, such as our leaders.

So what I propose to do is quote from just one of the sermons of Bishop von Galen, from which we may gain instruction in this regard. The sermon is below:

Sermon Delivered by
Bishop Clemens August
Count of Galen on August 3, 1941[1]

The Third Sermon, preached in the Church of St. Lambert's on August 3rd, 1941 in which the Bishop attacks the Nazi practice of euthanasia and condemns the 'mercy killings' taking place in his own diocese. Note: Some words were printed in boldface by this website.

My Beloved Brethren,

In today's Gospel we read of an unusual event: Our Saviour weeps. Yes, the Son of God sheds tears. Whoever weeps must be either in physical or mental anguish. At that time Jesus was not yet in bodily pain and yet

---

[1] Source: From the book *Cardinal von Galen* by Rev. Heinrich Portmann, translated by R.L. Sedgwick, 1957, pp. 239-246.

here were tears. What depth of torment He must have felt in His heart and Soul, if He, the bravest of men, was reduced to tears. Why is He weeping? He is lamenting over Jerusalem, the holy city He loved so tenderly, the capital of His race. He is weeping over her inhabitants, over His own compatriots because they cannot foresee the judgment that is to overtake them, the punishment which His divine prescience and justice have pronounced. 'Ah, if thou too couldst understand, above all in this day that is granted thee, the ways that can bring thee peace!' Why did the people of Jerusalem not know it? Jesus had given them the reason a short time before. 'Jerusalem, Jerusalem how often have I been ready to gather thy children together, as a hen gathers her chickens under her wings; and thou didst refuse it! I your God and your King wished it, but you would have none of Me.' This is the reason for the tears of Jesus, for the tears of God. Tears for the misrule, the injustice and man's willful refusal of Him and the resulting evils, which, in His divine omniscience, He foresees and which in His justice He must decree. It is a fearful thing when man sets his will against the will of God, and it is because of this that Our Lord is lamenting over Jerusalem.

My faithful brethren! In the pastoral letter drawn up by the German Hierarchy on the 26th of June at Fulda and appointed to be read in all the churches of Germany on July 6th, it is expressly stated: **'According to Catholic doctrine, there are doubtless commandments which are not binding when obedience to them requires too great a sacrifice, but there are sacred obligations of conscience from which no one can release us and which we must fulfil even at the price of death itself. At no time, and under no circumstances whatsoever, may a man, except in war and in lawful defence, take the life of an innocent person.'**

When this pastoral was read on July 6th I took the opportunity of adding this exposition:

For the past several months it has been reported that, on instructions from Berlin, **patients who have been suffering for a long time from apparently incurable diseases have been forcibly removed from homes and clinics. Their relatives are later informed that the patient has died, that the body has been cremated and that the ashes may be claimed. There is little doubt that these numerous cases of unexpected death in the case of the insane are not natural, but often deliberately caused, and result from the belief that it is lawful to take away life which is unworthy of being lived.**

This ghastly doctrine tries to justify the murder of blameless men and would seek to give legal sanction to the forcible killing of invalids, cripples, the incurable and the incapacitated. I have discovered that the practice here in Westphalia is to compile lists of such patients who are to be removed elsewhere as **'unproductive citizens,'** and after a period of time put to death. This very week, the first group of these patients has been sent from the clinic of Marienthal, near Münster.

Paragraph 21 of the Code of Penal Law is still valid. It states that anyone who deliberately kills a man by a premeditated act will be executed as a murderer. It is in order to protect the murderers of these poor invalids—members of our own families—against this legal punishment, that the patients who are to be killed are transferred from their domicile to some distant institution. Some sort of disease is then given as the cause of death, but as cremation immediately follows it is impossible for either their families or the regular police to ascertain whether death was from natural causes.

I am assured that at the Ministry of the Interior and at the Ministry of Health, no attempt is made to hide the fact that a great number of the insane have already been deliberately killed and that many more will follow.

Article 139 of the Penal Code expressly lays down that anyone who knows from a reliable source of any plot against the life of a man and who does not inform the proper authorities or the intended victim, will be punished.

When I was informed of the intention to remove patients from Marienthal for the purpose of putting them to death I addressed the following registered letter on July 29th to the Public Prosecutor, the Tribunal of Münster, as well as to the Head of the Münster Police:

'I have been informed this week that a considerable number of patients from the provincial clinic of Marienthal are to be transferred as citizens alleged to be **"unproductive"** to the institution of Richenberg, there to be executed immediately; and that according to general opinion, this has already been carried out in the case of other patients who have been removed in like manner. Since this sort of procedure is not only contrary to moral law, both divine and natural, but is also punishable by death, according to Article 211 of the Penal Code, it

is my bounden obligation in accordance
with Article 139 of the same Code to inform
the authorities thereof. Therefore I demand
at once protection for my fellow country-
men who are threatened in this way, and
from those who purpose to transfer and kill
them, and I further demand to be informed
of your decision.'

I have received no news up till now of any
steps taken by these authorities. On July
26th I had already written and dispatched a
strongly worded protest to the Provincial
Administration of Westphalia which is re-
sponsible for the clinics to which these patients have been entrusted for care and
treatment. My efforts were of no avail. The
first batch of innocent folk have left Marienthal under sentence of death, and I am informed that no less than eight hundred cases
from the institution of Wainstein have now
gone. And so we must await the news that
these wretched defenceless patients will
sooner or later lose their lives. Why? Not because they have committed crimes worthy of

death, not because they have attacked guardians or nurses as to cause the latter to defend themselves with violence which would be both legitimate and even in certain cases necessary, like killing an armed enemy soldier in a righteous war.

No, these are not the reasons why these unfortunate patients are to be put to death. It is simply because that **according to some doctor, or because of the decision of some committee, they have no longer a right to live because they are 'unproductive citizens'.** The opinion is that since they can no longer make money, they are obsolete machines, comparable with some old cow that can no longer give milk or some horse that has gone lame. What is the lot of unproductive machines and cattle? They are destroyed. I have no intention of stretching this comparison further. The case here is not one of machines or cattle which exist to serve men and furnish them with plenty. They may be legitimately done away with when they can no longer fulfil their function.

Here we are dealing with human beings, with our neighbours, brothers and sisters, the poor and invalids unproductive— perhaps! But have they, therefore, lost the right to live? Have you or I the right to exist only because we are 'productive'? If the principle is established that unproductive human beings may be killed, then God help all those invalids who, in order to produce wealth, have given their all and sacrificed their strength of body. If all unproductive people may thus be violently eliminated, then woe betide our brave soldiers who return home, wounded, maimed or sick.

Once admit the right to kill unproductive persons then none of us can be sure of his life. We shall be at the mercy of any committee that can put a man on the list of unproductives. There will be no police protection, no court to avenge the murder and inflict punishment upon the murderer. Who can have confidence in any doctor? He has but to certify his patients as unproductive and he receives the command to kill. If this dreadful doctrine is permitted and practised it is impossible to conjure up the degradation to which it will lead. Suspicion and distrust will be sown within the family itself. **A curse on men and on the German people if we break the holy commandment 'Thou shalt not kill'** which was given us by God on Mount Sinai with thunder and lightning, and which God our Maker imprinted on the human conscience from the beginning of time! Woe to us German people if we not only licence this heinous offence but allow it to be committed with impunity!

I will now give you a concrete example of what is taking place here. A fifty-five-year-old peasant from a country parish near Münster—I could give you his name—has been cared for in the clinic of Marienthal for some years suffering from some mental derangement. He was not hopelessly mad, in fact he could receive visitors and was always pleased to see his family. About a fortnight ago he had a visit from his wife and a soldier son who was home on leave from the front.

The latter was devoted to his sick father. Their parting was sad, for they might not see each other again as the lad might fall in battle. As it happens this son will never set eyes on his father again because he is on the list of the 'unproductives'. A member of the family who was sent to see the father at Marienthal was refused admission and was informed that the patient had been taken away on the orders of the Council of Ministers of National Defence. His whereabouts was unknown. The family would receive official notification in due course. What will this notice contain? Will it be like all the others, namely that the man is dead and that the ashes of his body will be sent on the receipt of so much money to defray expenses? And so the son who is now risking his life at the front for his German compatriots will never again see his father. These are the true facts and the names of all those concerned are available.

'Thou shalt not kill.' God engraved this commandment on the souls of men long before any penal code laid down punishment for murder, long before any court prosecuted and avenged homicide. Cain, who killed his brother Abel, was a murderer long before courts or states came into existence, and plagued by his conscience he confessed, 'Guilt like mine is too great to find forgiveness and I shall wander over the earth, a fugitive; anyone I meet will slay me.'

Because of His love for us God has engraved these commandments in our hearts and has made them manifest to us. They express the need of our nature created by God. They are the unchangeable and fundamental truths of our social life grounded on reason, well pleasing to God, healthful and sacred. God, Our Father, wishes by these precepts to gather us, His children, about Him as a hen shelters her brood under her wings. If we are obedient to His commands, then we are protected and preserved against the destruction with which we are menaced, just as the chicks beneath the wings of the mother. 'Jerusalem, Jerusalem how often have I been ready to gather thy children together, as a hen gathers her chickens under her wings; and thou didst refuse it!'

Does history again repeat itself here in Germany, in our land of Westphalia, in our city of Münster? Where in Germany and where, here, is obedience to the precepts of God? The eighth commandment requires 'Thou shalt not bear false witness against thy neighbour'. How often do we see this commandment publicly and shamelessly broken? In the seventh commandment we read, 'Thou shalt not steal'. But who can say that property is safe when our brethren, monks and nuns, are forcibly and violently despoiled of their convents, and who now protects property if it is illegally sequestered and not given back?

The sixth commandment tells us, 'Thou shalt not commit adultery'. Consider the instructions and assurances laid down on the question of free love and child-bearing outside the marital law in the notorious open letter of Rudolf Hess, who has since vanished, which appeared in the Press. In this respect look at the immorality and indecency everywhere in Münster today. Our young people have little respect for the propriety of dress today. Thus is modesty, the custodian of purity, destroyed, and the way for adultery lies open.

How do we observe the fourth commandment which enjoins obedience and respect to parents and superiors? Parental authority is at a low ebb and is constantly being enfeebled by the demands made upon youth against the wishes of the parents. How can real respect and conscientious obedience to the authority of the State be maintained, to say nothing of the Divine commandments, if one is fighting against the one and only true God and His Faith?

The first three commandments have long counted for nothing in the public life of Germany and here also in Münster. The Sabbath is desecrated; Holy Days of Obligation are secularized and no longer observed in the service of God. His name is made fun of, dishonoured and all too frequently blasphemed. As for the first commandment, 'Thou shalt not have strange gods before me', instead of the One, True, Eternal God, men have created at the dictates of their whim, their own gods to adore Nature, the State, the Nation or the Race. In the words of St. Paul, for many their god is their belly, their ease, to which all is sacrificed down to conscience and honour for the gratification of the carnal senses, for wealth and ambition. Then we are not surprised that they should claim divine privileges and seek to make themselves overlords of life and death.

'And as He drew near, and caught sight of the city, He wept over it, and said: "Ah, if thou too couldst understand, above all in this day that is granted thee, the ways that can bring thee peace! As it is, they are hidden from thy sight. The days will come upon thee when thy enemies will fence thee round about, and encircle thee, and press thee hard on every side, and bring down in ruin both thee and thy children that are in thee, not leaving one stone of thee upon another; and all because thou didst not recognize the time of My visiting thee".'

Jesus saw only the walls and towers of the city of Jerusalem with His human eye, but with His divine prescience He saw far beyond and into the inmost heart of the city and its inhabitants. He saw its wicked obstinacy, terrible, sinful and cruel. Man, a transitory creature, was opposing his mean will to the Will of God. That is the reason why Jesus wept for this fearful sin and its inevitable punishment. God is not mocked.

Christians of Münster! Did the Son of God in His omniscience see only Jerusalem and its people? Did He weep only on their behalf? Is God the protector and Father of the Jews only? Is Israel alone in rejecting His divine truth? Are they the only people to throw off the laws of God and plunge headlong to ruin? Did not Jesus, Who sees everything, behold also our German people, our land of Westphalia and the Lower Rhine, and our city of Münster? Has He not also wept for us? For a thousand years He has instructed us and our forbears in the Faith. He has led us by His law. He has nourished us with His grace and has gathered us to Him as the hen does her brood beneath its wings. Has the all-knowing Son of God seen that in our own time He would have to pronounce on us that same dread sentence? 'Not leaving one stone of thee upon another; and all because thou didst not recognize the time of My visiting thee.' That would indeed be a terrible sentence.

My dearly Beloved, I trust that it is not too late. It is time that we realized today what alone can bring us peace, what alone can save us and avert the divine wrath. We must openly, and without reserve, admit our Catholicism. We must show by our actions that we will live our lives by obeying God's commandments. Our motto must be: Death rather than sin. By pious prayer and penance we can bring down upon us all, our city and our beloved German land, His grace and forgiveness.

But those who persist in inciting the anger of God, who revile our Faith, who hate His commandments, who associate with those who alienate our young men from their religion, who rob and drive out our monks and nuns, who condemn to death our innocent brothers and sisters, our fellow human beings, we shun absolutely so as to remain undefiled by their blasphemous way of life, which would lay us open to that just punishment which God must and will inflict upon all those who, like the thankless Jerusalem, oppose their wishes to those of God.

O my God, grant to us all now on this very day, before it is too late, a true realization of the things that are for peace. O Sacred Heart of Jesus, oppressed even unto tears by the blindness and sins of men, help us by Thy grace to seek always what is pleasing to Thee and reject what is displeasing, so that we may dwell in Thy Love and find rest in our souls. Amen.

What a message to his beloved Catholic flock in the diocese of Munster! But he also addressed it to all of his beloved nation Germany, enslaved then under the cruel and godless rule of Hitler and the Nazis. The homily goes through all the Commandments and points out how each of them had been flouted in the recent history of the nation. He focuses however on the fifth and targets a State policy that purposely directed the killing of vulnerable innocent human beings, as not useful or "productive" any longer to the nation. The brazenness of this leads him to bring out the background of breaches of all the other commandments of God, which were also sins against the natural moral law and radically irrational. In fact, this sinful condition had worked its way into the fabric and culture of the modern State.

We all know how the Nazi State quickly descended to a level of murder and lies that would have destroyed it even if it was not defeated militarily. The irrational hatred and insane attempt to carry out the extermination of the Jewish people under its control was but the most horrible part of this self-destructive political program. The bishop's mind at this time, for reasons that we need not speculate, was not turned to the situation of the Jews, even though their condition clearly came within the subject he was directly dealing with; the horrific policy of exterminating whoever was regarded as unfit from the viewpoint of the Nazi State.

Bishop von Galen struck at the root of the sinful condition, which he saw as fallen man regarding his will as absolute and free to determine who was not fit to live and thus deserving of death. With the gaining of political power such an irrational individual, of which Hitler was the type, sought to rule his nation and if possible the whole world.

What strikes us today is how his description of the state of German society, which he relates to that of the Chosen People who had rejected Christ and therefore God, is a picture of the state of every society and State today, worst in that part of the world that was formerly Christian, or the "West".

We could take each of the commandments dealt with by the bishop and point out the rejection of the divinely revealed law (based also in the Natural Moral Law). We would note in each case a consequent flouting with ever increasing intensity, a march in triumph as it were by the Malignus himself. The deterioration in social morality and civic honesty is all too obvious to detail; the idea of obedience to God mocked, honour to parents forgotten, respect for human life lost, the most vulnerable and innocent murdered in millions, the natural institutions of marriage and the family set aside for exultation in the most disgraceful pleasures of unnatural sexual acts; the natural institution of property abused by the very governments obliged to protect it, and the world of commerce overtaken by the love of money for its own sake (the root of all evil); and on top of this the social order of communication immersed in a sea of lies and deceit. Propaganda in the media and corruption in politics is taken almost as normal.

But we will focus, as bishop von Galen did, on the flouting of the fifth commandment. In order to do this we insert here a short extract from St. Thomas on the Fifth Commandment.

Extract from St. Thomas on the Fifth Commandment in his "Explanation of the Ten Commandments"

"You Shall Not Kill." THE SIN OF KILLING

In the divine law which tells us we must love God and our neighbor, it is commanded that we not only do good but also avoid evil. The greatest evil that can be done to one's neighbor is to take his life. This is prohibited in the Commandment: "You shall not kill."

Killing of Animals Is Lawful.—In connection with this Commandment there are three errors. Some have said that it is not permitted to kill even brute animals. But this is false, because it is not a sin to use that which is subordinate to the power of man. It is in the natural order that plants be the nourishment of animals, certain animals nourish others, and all for the nourishment of man: "Even the green herbs have I delivered them all to you" [Gen 9:3]. The Philos-

opher says that hunting is like a just war
[*Politics* I]. And St. Paul says: "Whatsoever is
sold in the meat market, eat; asking no ques-
tions for conscience' sake" [1 Cor 10:25].
Therefore, the sense of the Commandment
is: "You shall not kill men."

The Execution of Criminals.—Some
have held that the killing of man is prohibited altogether. They believe that judges in the
civil courts are murderers, who condemn
men to death according to the laws. Against
this St. Augustine says that God by this
Commandment does not take away from
Himself the right to kill. Thus, we read: "I
will kill and I will make to live" [Deut 32:39].
It is, therefore, lawful for a judge to kill according to a mandate from God, since in this
God operates, and every law is a command
of God: "By Me kings reign, and lawgivers
decree just things" [Prov 8:15]. And again:
"For if you do what is evil, fear; for he does
not bear the sword in vain; for he is God's
minister" [Rm 13:14]. To Moses also it was
said: "Wizards you shall not allow to live"

[Ex 22:18]. And thus that which is lawful to God is lawful for His ministers when they act by His mandate. It is evident that God who is the Author of laws, has every right to inflict death on account of sin. For "the wages of sin is death" [Rm 6:23]. Neither does His minister sin in inflicting that punishment. The sense, therefore, of "You shall not kill" is that one shall not kill by one's own authority.

Suicide is Prohibited.—There are those who held that although this Commandment forbids one to kill another, yet it is lawful to kill oneself. Thus, there are the examples of Samson (Judges, xvi) and Cato and certain virgins who threw themselves into the flames, as St. Augustine relates in *The City of God* [I, 27]. But he also explains this in the words: "He who kills himself, certainly kills a man" [*ibid*. 13]. If it is not lawful to kill except by the authority of God, then it is not lawful to kill oneself except either upon the authority of God or instructed by the Holy

Spirit, as was the case of Samson. Therefore, "you shall not kill."

Other Meanings of "To Kill."—It ought to be known that to kill a man may happen in several ways. Firstly, by one's own hand: "Your hands are full of blood" [Is 1:15]. This is not only against charity, which tells us to love our neighbor as ourself: "No murderer has eternal life abiding in himself" [Jn 3:15]. But also it is against nature, for "every beast loves its like" [Sir 13:19]. And so it is said: "He who strikes a man with a will to kill him, shall be put to death" [Ex 21:12]. He who does this is more cruel than the wolf, of which Aristotle says that one wolf will not eat of the flesh of another wolf [*De anima.* IV].

Secondly, one kills another by word of mouth. This is done by giving counsel to anyone against another by provocation, accusation, or detraction: "The sons of men whose teeth are weapons and arrows, and their tongue a sharp sword" [Ps 56:5]. Thirdly, by lending aid, as it is written: "My son, do not go with them ... for their feet run to evil, and they rush to shed blood" [Prov 1:15-16]. Fourthly, by consent: "They are worthy of death, not only they who do such things, but they also who consent to those who do them" [Rm 1:32]. Lastly, one kills another by giving a partial consent when the act could be completely prevented: "Deliver those who are led to death" [Prov 24:11]; or, if one can prevent it, yet does not do so through negligence or avarice. Thus, St. Ambrose says: "Give food to him that is dying of hunger; if you do not, you are his murderer."

We will make some comments on what St. Thomas says. The very last sentence as we read the situation is directly applicable to the starvation occurring in Gaza with the Israeli State forces (Defence!) unbelievingly blocking aid to the Palestinian people as they, mothers and children amongst them, die of starvation. Virtually the whole world, apart from the USA, pleads to let aid in with those who as St. Thomas citing St. Ambrose states are to be regarded as committing murder. How can the Israeli forces be allowed to do this? Only because they know that they have the backing of the USA (Big Brother). The action or inaction of the USA then falls into one or other of the indirect meanings of to kill or murder; given above by St. Thomas: e.g. by lending aid to a murderer and/or giving partial consent when the act could be completely prevented.

So it is that even by not having blood on their hands as the Israeli forces otherwise have in mass slaughter of innocent Palestinians (the numbers are horrific,) the USA is guilty of murder in these other ways as explained by St. Thomas. They will have to face their judgment on the day of reckoning.

Apart from these considerations relevant to the situation in Gaza St. Thomas deals with other issues to do with the fifth commandment which are not well understood even by today's Catholics. We pass over the specious argument used by animal liberationists such as Peter Singer that "not to kill" applies to more than human beings. This is answered in the first part of the quote from St. Thomas.

The next part involves the issue of capital punishment which is a vexed one and quite confusing with the change made to the Catechism in the last pontificate. This we believe arises because of a deeper confusion with regard to Ethics generally. Most of all, attention is not paid to how St. Thomas explains the words. "The sense, therefore, of "You shall not kill" is that one shall not kill by one's own authority". Only the Creator is the Lord of life and death of human creatures, to some of whom he gives such authority.

Some are upset by the Old Testament stories of slaughter of whole peoples and equate this with modern mass murder. But the solution is simple if one understands that what is wrong for man is not wrong for God or for those he authorises. St. Thomas gives examples of the latter. We need not go any further into this. Though it is something the modern mind makes much of. So too is it not difficult to resolve the problem of capital punishment. The natural institutions of civil communities may be at least assumed to have the power to do what is necessary for the common good of the community. But this is not to be thought of as a power in political governments to execute criminals on their own authority. That is where the modern problem of capital punishment comes in.

Human society or its legislators and judges have no power or right to kill anyone if they do not have that authority from God. The problem cases may be solved in this way. For St. Thomas, and for one who acknowledges the existence and authority of God, the right to punish criminals even by capital punishment may be allowed to civil governments. If it may be assumed that they act from divine authority (indeed, all authority and power is from God). There may be some difficulty distinguishing the natural from the supernatural. We will not go into the necessary distinctions to be observed, especially between just and unjust laws.

A peculiar problem arises in modern times, however, where the divine authority of the Catholic Church has been explicitly rejected by Protestant and secularist States. With this necessarily goes rejection of the Natural Moral Law where the divine authority naturally comes from. This is confirmed by Scripture. Without Faith it is impossible to please God.

It is clear from modern history that modern society immediately began to decline morally and has now reached a condition of immorality and irreligion that is terminal. In terms of legal and political philosophy this can be seen in the advocacy of legal positivism and of regarding political authority as based on purely human power which is indeed reduced to brute force. There is no notion of natural law and natural justice. As both St. Augustine and St. Thomas say, an unjust law is not law but a species of violence. It should be understood that legal positivism is the theory of law taught generally in the leading countries of the West such as USA, UK and Australia. Corresponding to this is the theory of political authority based on the State possessing absolute power.

What Bishop von Galen saw come out in Germany was only the putting into practice of modern legal and political philosophy in its most virulent form. The rejection of divine authority is the root of the desire to destroy the Catholic Church, not just in Nazism but generally in the Western world ("Western Civilisation"). For the Church is the only institution that stands in the way of the vision of the State as absolute.

Legal positivism is the philosophy of law which is applied in modern courts. There may be a constitution written or unwritten that puts certain limits on current human legislators and judges. But these constitutions are human documents or conventions. So too are the precedents of former decisions by courts taken as authority that binds them. The notion that civil (and criminal) laws depend upon divine authority, or fundamentally upon natural moral law and natural justice is rejected, at times scornfully. As Bishop von Galen noted this equated with the notion of the State as absolute. Its will expressed by a single individual or "a majority 'in Parliament assembled'" is the ultimate basis of the law's force.

So we have the problem of upon what authority does a modern State rule over its subjects. It is clear that acting on its own authority it has no right to kill any of them, whether criminal or not. And since all power and authority is from God, a civil society that officially denies any dependence upon divine authority undermines all its authority and power and necessarily falls back on enforcing obedience and compliance with its will (individual or collective) by brute force. This is what the modern political theories of Niccolo Machiavelli and Thomas Hobbes come to. It is from this "realpolitik" position that they have their celebrated position in the modern theory of law and politics. It is this legal positivist theory (denying any natural law) that is generally taught and held in the modern legal, judicial and political law schools in countries in the West, led by the UK and the USA.

There are complications in judging individual cases. First of all, there is the continued influence of the Catholic Church from which much good flows into the civil societies despite the attacks on it and the rejection of the moral law it protects. There are members of Catholic laity as well who fill the ranks of politicians and lawyers, many of whom rise to high positions in government and judiciary. Their influence, however, is mixed, for their education in the basic secularist theories of law and politics is powerful, leading some astray even morally in all three orders, personal (religious), domestic and political. We need not name individual cases even at the level of presidents and prime ministers.

Jeffrey Sachs, an American Jew, has noted a curious thing about the Zionist claim to have divine warrant for the takeover of the lands occupied by Palestinians adjacent to the current boundaries of Israel. He notes that Zionism is a movement among American Christians rather than American Jews. The reason for this may appear from what we have noted above.

From a Christian/Catholic position, however, it needs to be noted that the divine support of the Jews as a nation passed away with their rejection of the true Messiah, Jesus Christ. There is no preferential status of divine grace now for any part of humanity, nor any basis for a claim to a particular portion of the lands of the earth. So the Zionist claim to a particular territory in the region of former Israel by divine donation is false.

It is all but impossible to determine property rights in the history of humanity. For distributive justice in this regard is politically corrupted by robbery on a grand scale. The peoples of the world have to cope as best they can with apportionment that exists. At the merely human level one oligarchical empire generally succeeds another, and the present times are no different.

On this score alone the prospects for peace and unity which all men of good will long for are rather grim, even less so than during Bishop von Galen's time.

However, having survived such a horrific period of mass slaughter and suffering the world thought good times were ahead. It is hard to believe that we are in the new 21st century within a period that is worse in many ways. We have only to compare the evils of sinful rejection of God's law and love that the bishop lists in his homily, taking the Commandments one by one with the current state of the world. We will come back to the fifth commandment. We will not go into the first three as blasphemy is a forgotten concept. What von Galen noted about lack of honour to one's parents has worsened. The notion of the natural institution of family hardly exists any more. Was the institution of marriage in von Galen's Germany so perverted as it is now? Lies and propaganda have abounded since before modern society and the Nazis made great use of them. But present day misuse of media communication in commerce, politics and war has the advantage of advanced technology that Goebbels could only have dreamed of.

As we have noticed Jeffrey Sachs is a permanent member of the Pontifical Academy of Social Sciences. He was appointed by Pope Francis. He has claimed that he used to meet weekly with the pope to confer on the world situation of multiple conflicts and efforts for dialogue and peace. He is probably the most expert of all the members of the Academy with an intimate knowledge of world affairs both nationally of his own country and internationally of all countries involved in current conflicts, going back to before the fall of the Soviet Union. He is one of the most severe critics, if not the most severe, of the policies and actions of both the State of Israel and the US. His condemnation of both has grown more damning in recent days, as anyone who views his public appearances will know. It is quite evident that he is a person of extraordinary courage, fortified by a righteous anger at the crimes he sees committed by the State of Israel and "assisted" by the US. We wonder if Pope Leo XIV has conferred with him, especially on what he regards as the complicity of America in Israel's war crimes, "ethnic cleansing" and genocide of Palestinians in Gaza?

There are differences of course between the situation with which Bishop von Galen was faced and the present situation. We will go into this. But we contend that what von Galen says in his homily with respect to sins by the government against the fifth commandment can be readily applied to the current circumstances involving the State of Israel and the US and indeed virtually all States in what we call Western Civilisation.

Let us look at the differences. Bishop von Galen was primarily focused on his own Catholic diocese, in the context of his own country Germany. Coming from an aristocratic family he was fiercely proud of his nation with the politics of which members of his family were deeply concerned, filling important posts in government. This connection with the government of Germany disappeared with the dismantling of the aristocratic element in German society after the First World War. Nonetheless, von Galen remained a solid patriot and defended the shift to a more democratic form of government, even defending initially that of Hitler. He was soon to be disabused in this regard and condemned in the strongest terms what he saw as sins against the fifth commandment of the most vile kind. Our interest is not in the position of a bishop as caught up in his nation that has gone rogue and is guilty directly of mass slaughter of its own citizens, but of bishops caught up with States which are indirectly guilty as explained by St. Thomas. We are concerned with States which fit into that category of sin against murder, with particular focus on the US. The citizens, including bishops, of the United States are just as patriotic as Bishop von Galen was of his country. He found it necessary to condemn the actions of his own country. Do the bishops of the US find the same necessity?

We are not so much concerned with the actions of citizens of the State of Israel in the matter. We will let people read Peter Beinart's book and come to their own view on that. Our main interest is in the sense of responsibility of American Catholics and especially their leaders.

Bishop von Galen and his family were devout Catholics and well schooled in their Faith and moral doctrine, seeing their privileged position as carrying with it a great responsibility in works of justice and charity.

The vehemence and savagery of the Hitler regime no doubt came as a shock to him. However, he soon came to see the underlying causes of the descent into evil. We can see that expressed in his homily.

The moral state of Germany, as with the rest of Europe, and extending to the whole of modern "Western Civilisation" had eroded at a very fundamental level. This however was a gradual process, hidden somewhat by the celebration of the enormous "progress" in science and technology that had occurred at the same time.

As we have seen in our previous books, the notion of science had changed from that of premodern times, and in a way that meant a loss of wisdom, both natural and practical as we have explained. The loss of natural wisdom, which may be connected with Aristotle's concept of Metaphysics (which is also Metamathematics) was the most fundamental. It went unnoticed in the elevation of Mathematics to the place of the supreme science. But more immediately deleterious to social and political life was the loss of practical wisdom, which as a science was known to Aristotle and Aquinas as Ethics. A necessary understanding of Morality and the Natural Moral Law was thereby lost. Again this went somewhat un-noticed as technology took the place of practical science and its spectacular advances overshadowed the gradual but steep decline in morals. The great advances in medicine are a prime example here. It is all but forgotten that the science of medicine, though a practical science, is not an ethical but a technical one, which Aristotle and Aquinas knew as of the higher kind cooperative with nature. As completed by an art it has virtually taken the place of the moral virtue of prudence. The notion of "safe sex" is a case in point. It seems to imply right conduct, but it does not. The same thing happens with the art of psychiatry. Sexual acts are moral only in the institution of marriage but are treated as to be considered only at the level of bodily health and pleasure the same as that of animals.

Bishop von Galen relates the moral decline to the rejection of the Commandments, which inevitably followed from the rejection of faith in, and moral authority of, the Catholic Church. He was also able to relate it to the modern political theory of the State as absolute.

What is to be noted is that the deterioration particularly in regard to moral and political affairs was not confined to Germany, nor to Europe, but was a general condition of modern society in "Western Civilization' after the revolutionary break with the Catholic Church at the beginning of the modern era. This was quite radical and seemingly total, but the revolutionary elements have come and gone and the Church has survived, if as Chesterton puts it, "reeling but erect".

We do not intend to go into historical details here. The philosophical explanations are dealt with in our previous books. What we wish to focus on here is the application of the moral judgment made by Bishop von Galen in regard to the situation in Nazi Germany to the attitude of bishops in the US to the culpability of their own nation in the present "war" in Gaza. We will come to extend this to other States in the "West" who support the State of Israel and follow the lead of the US.

There is this difference then between the situation Bishop von Galen faced in his country's sinning against the fifth commandment being in the direct murder of its citizens and the situation that the US bishops face in the US sinning against the fifth commandment in another way as we have discussed. But there is no real difference in the fact that both are faced with the same sin of State sponsored murder of fellow human beings. The American bishops (and others in the West) who are silent or supportive carry the same responsibility to protest and condemn as did Bishop von Galen. How many do so?

Though he is an American citizen the pope seems to be in a different position as his responsibility is of much wider scope. He would have to consider repercussions as Pope Pius XII did. Yet for one thing it seems that the leaders of Israel and the US are not as likely to react so insanely as Hitler, nor do they have the same ability as the Nazis had in the Netherlands. Public condemnation therefore seems to be called for with regard to both the State of Israel and the US.

Sins against the fifth commandment are of course not the only serious ones committed by nations. But, as St. Thomas notes, to kill that amounts to murder is the most evil thing that one can do to one's fellow man at the level of ordinary justice.

We should say something, however, about the other offences against the Ten Commandments to put things in context. The first three are of most importance and the fourth a serious obligation. But we can leave them to another work.

The other six focus on injustice to one's neighbour but we can limit or comment on them to four as the last two are related to the sixth and seventh. These four are murder, adultery, theft and false witness or lying. We have no need to explain the depth of evil connected with the fifth and eighth as the devil is called a murderer from the beginning and the father of lies. It might be noticed that we are dealing with the moral virtue of justice, not truth as such, in the case of the eighth commandment. It is concerned with truth-telling as a matter of justice to one's fellow human beings. The misuse of language plays a central role in the work of the devil.

The sixth and seventh need some further explanation as there are two levels of the natural moral law on which they have to be considered. Both have natural institutions that regulate the goodness of human relations in their regard, marriage in the case of the sixth commandment and property in the case of the seventh. Neither of these are well understood in modern moral discussion, and the confusion there plays into the hands of all evildoers. Both institutions pre-date the formation of civil societies and so the governments of States have a fundamental obligation to protect them.

There is a basic obligation to apportion the lands and other natural resources in the territory concerned according to distributive justice and the needs of the common good. It is plain from history that this is rarely if ever done and those in power have favoured their own. There is great disproportion in the distribution, giving some (the powerful and their favoured) unfair advantage over others.

In modern times this already disordered situation was made much worse by wholesale plunder and robbery by those who usurped power, in the "West", following the fall of Christian civilization called Christendom.

A close study of history reveals that this division took the form of a division between Capital and Labour, as a short description for the few excessively rich coming to have virtual control of all property and the majority poor (workers) reduced to a state of having little or no property or "capital". The workers were reduced to a condition of proletarianism, as Pope Leo XIII stated in *Rerum novarum*, bearing a yoke little better than slavery.

This was alleviated to some extent by individual works of charity and a sense of justice even in some rich. But the system was such, as we have explained in our books on the subject, that it inexorably led to Charles Dickens' picture of "industrial" relations described in his book "Hard Times" (the schoolmaster given the name "Gradgrind").

Pope Leo's first modern social encyclical led to an awakening of Western social conscience in this regard but there was also the collapse of this unbridled Capitalist Economy in the Great Depression and two World Wars that forced the State to intervene. We should also mention the rise of Communism.

Unfortunately, any understanding of the natural character of the institution of property was totally lost in the war between two opposed ideologies that still exist. This conflict is even more complicated by the turn of diabolical assault on the natural institution of marriage.

In both the sixth and seventh commandments as we have noted we need to note a deeper level of sin than against property (theft) and against the marital relation. In regard to the former there is a fundamental obligation to respect an individual's right to access to the goods of the earth to preserve his own life. Anyone who prevents him in this regard and the person dies is guilty of murder as St. Ambrose says.

Adultery presupposes marriage (as theft does property). But more fundamental than this is the natural order of male and female where sexual relations are concerned. Underlying the seventh commandment as noted is the natural order of all men's right in case of necessity to access to the goods of the earth, whether in a raw or produced state.

The violation of the male/female nature of human sexual relations is as St. Thomas notes much graver than formication. It necessarily contradicts the most fundamental order of the act to reproduction of a human being, which marriage itself is ordered to fundamentally.

The malice of artificial contraceptive practice, as St. Thomas states, is "proximate to homicide". So both offenses are against natural law at a deeper level and approach the seriousness of murder.

Yet we see the modern world treat violation of these two commandments at this unnatural level lightly. They will not be so regarded on the day of reckoning. The Church cannot remain silent about their wickedness.

However, we wish to confine our attention to the fifth commandment and the modern violation of it. In a perverse way the turmoil to do with other commandments can be used to distract attention from attention to sins in regard to one. Focus on sins against the fifth commandment is obviously of the greatest importance. In the case of the Palestinians in Gaza there is a huge push to diminish its sinfulness and excuse the perpetrators of mass slaughter and starvation both direct and indirect.

Conclusion

This letter/article has been focused on sins against the fifth commandment Not to kill, which properly understood forbids murder.

This was the principal concern of Bishop von Galen in his homily quoted, though he dealt also with the other commandments and the modern violation of them. His condemnation was of direct murder by his own nation, Germany, under a deliberate policy of extermination by Hitler and the Nazis. He was concerned with the carrying out of this policy upon his own people before his very eyes. He does not refer in his homily to the mass murder of Jewish people; though it is clear that what he condemned included the killing of them.

All that he says can be applied generally to crimes of murder and we have quoted an extract from St. Thomas on the fifth commandment which shows that murder is to be understood in ways other than direct killing. We are mainly concerned with murder committed in other ways than directly as explained by St. Thomas.

This can be seen happening today in the support of the State of Israel by the US of what is a State policy of killing indiscriminately Palestinian people in Gaza including untold thousands of women and children - refer to the public statements of professors John Mearsheimer and Jeffrey Sachs above.

That obliges all to condemn not only the State of Israel but also the United States. People in America (US) are reluctant to do this for the reasons we have alluded to. To accuse Israel of such crime draws accusations of being antisemitic, which, with the Holocaust still within living memory is hard to counter. It is almost incomprehensible to imagine Jews as perpetrators of the same crime that so many suffered less than a century ago.

For most it would take a reading of Peter Beinart's book, and listening to Jeffrey Sachs and other Jews like Norman Finkelstein, to give the lie to such an accusation.

But the basic intent of this letter/article is to learn if there are bishops and Catholic clergy generally, especially US citizens, who are prepared to condemn their own nation/state as the Lion (Leo) of Munster Bishop von Galen did.